A Peek Into My Mind Palace

Sanhita Samant

BookLeaf
Publishing

India | USA | UK

Presentation by *BookLeaf Publishing*

Web: www.bookleafpub.com

E-mail: info@bookleafpub.com

ISBN: 9789363316225

First edition 2024

This book is dedicated to my late paternal grandfather, who brought the love of poetry in the household and indirectly inspired this book.

ACKNOWLEDGEMENT

I would like to start by thanking Aai and Baba for always being the biggest cheerleaders I could ask for. Without their encouragement, feedback and the discussions we have had, this book would not have been possible.

My dear friends who I have met both offline and online, thank you for all the hype and support! This broken girl was mended by your friendship.

Next, a big thank you to my English teacher, Mrs. Colaco, who made Shakespeare seem easy when we were struggling with the sonnets and plays and gave us in detailed analyses of ever complicated poems so that we wouldn't miss anything from what the poet wanted to say.

Miss Shradhanjali Tamang, my creative writing course professor, thank you for the detailed feedback on my assignments and the healthy environment you fostered in the course. Even though I was struggling with nervousness, you made it lighter.

There are a few other names that come to mind so I am going to sum it up by saying; thank you to the village that has been there for me while I struggled.

Last but not least, many thanks to BookLeaf Publishing for making this dream a reality.

PREFACE

Ever since I was little, I loved writing. I mostly wrote poems and short stories. A few years into school I lost the desire to write. Occasionally something would be written, but not the way I used to earlier. As I entered my twenties, it all started making a comeback. I even got the confidence to send my work to people I am close to, which I avoided out of fear. What if they laugh? What if they mock me? Obviously, making my work public was not even on my radar.

Last year, I took up a course on creative writing to better understand different writing styles, poems, fiction, etc. We had to make our work public and get a feedback from other classmates. It made me feel more confident. That is how the idea to publish a book was born.

I spend a lot of time in my mind palace. I think it is your turn now. This book of poems is your ticket to take a tour. Hope you enjoy!

Sisterhood

Sisters aren't always by blood,
Can't forget those who are your bud.
Who stand by you all the time,
Your cheerleaders, your partners in crime.

When I was little, I thought
Let's see what's in the classmate lot
It wasn't exactly the best,
To find traps in the nest.

My best friends by relation,
Became worse than my imagination,
When we entered our teens,
They forgot what sisterhood means.

What I thought were sleepover nights
Were opportunities to pick fights,
To belittle, tease and laugh at me,
Stopping me from being me.

Now with my new friends' support
And my Tartan sister acing the court,
I am reminded quite nicely,
You must never treat your 'sister' badly.

All I ask all 'sisters'
Is to not be like monsters,
To disagree but not dominate,
Try having a good relation, 'tis great!

Moving On

I still don't know when
I'll forget what was done then,
How am I to forget
Moments that made my eyes wet?

"Oh just move on", you say,
Like it doesn't affect me everyday,
Shut up, sorry to say,
It's not easy to put away!

I recollect every single thing
And they all still sting,
But I am getting better now,
I will heal, that is my vow.

Emotions Are Strange

I find it quite strange you know,
For people I never met, tears flow,
All I have are photographs,
And in the case of some, also autographs.

Seriously, emotions are so strange,
You can never predict their range!
At the same time you are confident
And fear you may cause an accident.

If at a moment you feel strong,
You also feel you don't belong,
But also, if you're feeling low,
One small gesture makes you glow.

In Law

There is a reason I say,
You won't hear of my wedding day,
From whatever I have heard and seen,
Wow, this new life can get so mean!

From the day you move in,
You have to have thick skin,
Because let me tell you,
Moments of joy will be few.

You will be told your food is bad,
You will get mocked, it'll make you mad,
Soon it will be a habit and make you sad,
Is there nothing kind to add?

In-law seems right,
You feel you're in a court alright!
Tossed and mocked constantly,
Be nice please, she's now your family!

The Tree Remembers

You've heard of the axe and the tree,
How the axe cuts and gets away scot-free,
The tree however, never forgets
The mental and physical pain it gets.

Shamelessly, the axe has the audacity
To act all happy and smiley,
How dare it smile at the tree!
Do not smile! Pay the fee!

When it is told it owes an apology,
It acts like a whiny baby,
That it is innocent, there's nothing wrong,
Must've been a misunderstanding all along.

The axe acts like all is okay,
The tree has never forgotten the day,
The axe is shameless, or really forgot,
The tree will never, absolutely not.

Genes

There's a big gap between two of my toes
And I have quite a wide nose,
My torso is significantly long,
Shoulders broad so I feel strong.

I have never ending curls in my hair,
For a face I have a circle there,
I have never done my eyebrows,
Saved myself from ah's and ow's.

All these features are from people I adore,
Features that are hard to ignore,
I would never let anyone call them ugly,
So maybe I should treat myself more nicely.

An Elegy On George Harrison

"Love one another", said he and breathed his
last,
One didn't think he would exit so fast,
As he went into a deep permanent sleep,
His guitars began to gently weep.

He was one of those individuals sent from
above,
To spread the message of peace and love,
He did his job pretty great you know,
So well that we were shattered when he had to
go.

Jade

You left the world early,
We miss you a ton, girly!
You said goodbye at twenty-seven,
In the summer of two thousand eleven.

Often when I'm in my bed,
Your songs run in my head,
That talk about waking up alone,
And how tears dry on their own.

You were stronger than me,
When I get criticism I want to flee,
Yes, I repeat, you were strong,
If you don't think so, you're wrong!

I am sorry we couldn't help you,
I really wish the world had saved you,
So you'd be here with us today,
With more music for us to play.

Double Standards

Why's it that being a fangirl
Makes the world go mad?
Fanboys are oh so cool,
But fangirls? That's bad!

You'll be questioned about teams and players,
To prove you really like that game of kicky
bally,
No one ever does that to fanboys,
Their support is taken seriously.

If you listen to classic rock,
"Name 3 albums", "Name so and so song"
Is what every boy will ask you,
Waiting to see if you get something wrong.

And if you do, oh the drama!
Not an error, you're a fake!
Okay. Happy? Delighted?
Do you want a cake?

Fanboys are never told,
"Get over this stupid phase."
Fangirls on the other hand,
Always seen as people with a craze.

Haiku Series 1: Feelings

[Confidence]
I found where it was,
Not in a place or a box,
It was within me.

[Her]
I miss who I was,
Carefree, not so anxious,
I want that again.

Haiku Series Part 2: Painters

[Van Gogh]
He painted all his life,
But no one cared until he,
Became one with dust.

[Impressionists]
They were rejected,
Their work was called incomplete,
Look who's laughing now!

Solo

I went to the City of Angels,
My first trip alone on a plane-
I know! I know! Me! Alone!
Accepting that this happened is insane.

For someone who once panicked
To call and place a food order,
How did she decide,
To fly past the Indian border?!

When I landed on Thai soil,
I almost shed a tear,
Did I really make it alone?
Without having any fear?

It felt so amazing
To explore a city all alone,
Getting validation from locals was a bonus
As you know the language skills were shown!

This trip proved that sometimes
The Universe does hear you,
I'd been wishing for this for years,
And am I glad it came true!

A Summer in Kenya

We decided to go to Kenya,
In the month of May,
I honestly can't remember,
When I had a bad day.

My eyes would feast
On the multicoloured sky,
My stomach and soul?
On every food item I walked by.

Every single day I felt like
I was on an episode of National Geographic,
The cherry on top was a balloon ride,
An experience oh so fantastic!

Actually, I lied,
That wasn't the cherry on top,
It was seeing baby elephants almost every day,
And me wishing time would stop.

Animal herds and birds,
Live and eat together in harmony,
And we call a bad person an animal,
Oh the irony!

Congratulations! It's A Girl!

The world's first author
Was a woman named Enheduanna,
Long division became easier,
Thanks to Ancient Alexandria's Hypatia.

In India, a multilingual poet
Was born in 1498 named Meera,
And the New World's first recorded feminist,
Was born in 1648 named Sor Juana.

In the Indian Rebellion Movement of 1857
The leading significant figure was Rani of
Jhansi,
And the same year she sacrificed her life,
Came India's first female scholar Pandita
Ramabai.

While in the United States of America
Harriet Tubman fought against slavery,
In Pune, India, Savitribai Phule
Fought to educate girls, I salute her bravery.

And let's not forget the contributions
Of Lise Meitner and Marie Curie,
And of course Rosalind Franklin,

The founder of DNA, forgotten brutally.

These and many other examples show us
That girls can do anything!
Open your mind, give us a platform,
You'll thank us for what we bring.

Someone's Someone

She is a daughter, a sister,
A wife and then a mother,
The circle of life goes on,
Then she's also a grandmother.

Yes, these titles are special,
But what about her own identity?
She has a name, a degree, a job,
Those things are forgotten conveniently.

Think on this a little,
Internal checks need to be done,
She is her own person,
Not just someone's someone.

Friendships

No idea about love that is romantic,
But I do know about the one that's platonic,
My friendships are my everything,
Oh! The comfort and joy they bring!

We discuss issues then and there,
Never thinking about how and where,
Thus a rug with unresolved issues doesn't exist,
Remember the more you wait, the bigger the list.

Some of my friendships did not last,
They exploded and remain in the past,
I however do not sit and mourn them,
As thankfully, there was nothing joyous about
'em.

Something I'd like to say,
If you're mistreated, do not stay!
You try and try to change so they like you,
No good in staying if you don't get to be you.

A Static Shock In Paris

I was in Paris heading out,
On a windy Thursday morning,
Little did I know that
I would soon be mourning.

Mourning the loss of you,
My dear dear friend,
I had just spoken to you,
Who knew that was the end?

The end of your time here,
On this planet we call home,
You chose to go in the skies,
Where you'd be freer to roam.

When I got your mum's text,
I thought there was an earthquake
In my head and around me,
And I felt hearts break.

The hearts of your friends,
Who had all got that text,
We're glad you felt we made you happy,
Till you went from one place to the next.

Mind Palace

Let us take a look,
At my mind palace,
Fasten your seatbelts!
It is a fascinating place.

First, the living room,
The absolute chaos!
Fashion, food and fandoms,
Too messy, let us cross.

Here in the corner,
Is a little storage place,
For anxiety and negativity
That want the whole place.

You have to be careful,
Those two are nasty!
While on your healing journey,
They interrupt- not so classy!

Out we go from this door,
There is this little pool,
You never know what's in it,
Who knows? A creativity jewel!

Last but so not the least,
The basement of the unconscious,
Randomly while I chill they pop up
And sheepishly ask "Remember us?"

Hey! Wait! Don't go!
Don't worry it's all okay!
It may seem scary and suspicious
But it's interesting in its own way.

From Me to Younger Me

Oh my broken, confused girl,
This poem is for you,
I am so so sorry
For all that you have been through.

People may have told you,
"Let go, it wasn't all that bad."
They are wrong, okay?
Nobody decides when you should be sad.

I know after all the pain,
You thought you are unworthy
Of friends, love and care,
You deserve it all! You hear girly?

I am here for you know,
I will make you happy,
I work to erase your sorrow,
Here's to no more feeling crappy.

A Thank You Note

Thank you to my parents
For helping me walk,
For being my first cheerleaders
And listening to me when I talk.

Thank you to my friends
For never judging me,
For all the laughs and advice,
And most importantly letting me be me.

Thank you to my teachers
For all that you have taught me,
Well, except those who yelled when
I tried expressing something freely.

And last but not the least,
To the people who left me,
Thank you! Thank you!
I needed that bad energy out badly!

Quarter

The day is coming soon,
That I complete a quarter century,
No idea what waits ahead,
Ah yes midlife crisis but first...party?

It feels like I've done a lot,
But also not that much,
But again I am an introvert
Who doesn't go out as such!

I think that younger me,
Would be very proud,
To know that though I'm quiet,
When needed I am now loud.

I strive to make her happy,
She needs to know it's all okay,
And the things that aren't yet,
Will certainly be one day.

www.ingramcontent.com/pod-product-compliance
Lightning Source LLC
Chambersburg PA
CBHW071241140726
47996CB00007B/2709